D1712522

AN ALBUM OF
TELEVISION

CAROL A. EMMENS

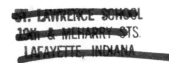
FRANKLIN WATTS | NEW YORK | LONDON | TORONTO | SYDNEY | 1980

Photographs courtesy of: RCA Corp.: pp. 2, 7; Bell Telephone: p. 4 (top and bottom left); General Electric Broadcasting Co.: p. 4 (bottom right); Roy Rogers: p. 8; Lone Ranger Television, Inc.: p. 10 (left); Gene Autry: p. 10 (right); Wisconsin Center for Film and Theater Research: pp. 13 (left and right), 24, 39 (bottom), 58 (right); NBC: pp. 14 (top and bottom), 21 (top and bottom), 28 (top), 39 (top), 48 (top), 76 (bottom left), 79 (top right); The Ed Sullivan Show: p. 17 (left); Arthur Godfrey: p. 17 (right); United Press International: p. 18 (top); Direct Recordings: p. 18 (bottom); Walt Disney Productions: p. 22; CBS: pp. 27, 31 (bottom right), 32 (left and bottom right), 54 (top right), 62 (left), 65 (top left and right), 69 (top and bottom), 72 (top); Richard Boone: p. 28 (bottom); George Burns: p. 31 (top); Bob Floper: p. 31 (bottom left); Lucille Ball Productions: p. 32 (top right); Columbia Pictures: p. 35; Warner Brothers Television: p. 36 (left); Lassie Television, Inc., A Subsidiary of Wrather Corp.: p. 36 (right); Bing Crosby Productions: pp. 40 (left), 61 (bottom right), 62 (bottom right); New York Public Library at Lincoln Center: p. 43 (top); Wide World Photos: p. 43 (bottom); Metro-Goldwyn-Mayer, Inc.: pp. 44, 62 (top right); Proctor and Gamble Productions: p. 47 (top left and right); ABC ©: pp. 47 (bottom), 51 (top left); New Yorker Films: p. 48 (bottom); Group W Productions: p. 51 (bottom); Carol Burnett: p. 52; Twentieth Century Fox: pp. 54 (left), 57 (top); Raymond Burr: p. 54 (bottom right); Paramount Pictures, Inc.: pp. 57 (bottom), 58 (left), 75 (top); Sheldon Leonard Productions: p. 58 (middle); Don Fedderson Productions: p. 61 (top left); Filmways, Inc.: p. 61 (bottom left and top right); Family Communications, Inc.: p. 65 (bottom left); Youngstreet Productions: p. 66 (top); Tom and Dick Smothers: p. 66 (bottom); Tandem Productions: p. 70; Henry Winkler: p. 72 (bottom); Wolper/Komak/Wannon Productions: p. 75 (bottom); Loriman Productions: p. 76 (top left); Spelling-Goldberg Productions: pp. 76 (top right), 79 (top left and bottom right); Children's Television Workshop ©: p. 80 (left and right); Public Broadcasting Service: p. 83 (left and top right); David Wolper Productions: pp. 83 (bottom right), 84 (top); Time Life Television: p. 84 (bottom).

Cover photograph of Lucille Ball courtesy of Lucille Ball Productions.

Library of Congress Cataloging in Publication Data

Emmens, Carol A
An album of television.

Bibliography: p.
Includes index.
SUMMARY: An overview of television and its influence in our daily lives from the first broadcasts of the 1930's to the present day.

1. Television broadcasting—United States—History—Juvenile literature. 2. Television programs—United States—Juvenile literature. [1. Television broadcasting—History. 2. Television programs] I. Title.
PN1992.3.U5E43   791.45′0973   79–22778
                ISBN 0–531–01503–3

#5154

CONTENTS

DEDICATED TO
MY SON, SCOTT,
WHO LOVES TELEVISION

ACKNOWLEDGMENTS

My thanks to Brian Camp,
the Educational Film Library Association;

David Hirsch, ABC Media Concepts;

Pat Diehl, CBS Entertainment;

the Television Information Office,
especially Leslie Slocum;

all the performers who provided photographs;

all the TV producers who cooperated;

and my family.

AN ALBUM OF TELEVISION

INTRODUCTION

Television entertains us, brings us the news, makes us laugh, and makes us cry. In the average American home, TV is on six hours a day. More people in the United States own TV sets than own refrigerators. There are 116 million sets, about one for every two people. And TV is only fifty years old.

Television influences what we buy to wear, to eat, and to use. By the time you are eighteen, you probably will have watched 350,000 commercials.

Political campaigns were changed by TV. Beginning with the first political speech on television, candidates worried about their TV image. Elections were revolutionized in 1952 when Dwight D. Eisenhower used one-minute spots to advertise himself during the presidential race.

Television brings the world into our living room— for 75 percent of us, in brilliant color.

Like the printing press, television revolutionized our lives.

Television pioneer Vladimir K. Zworykin holds an early model of an iconoscope, the "eye" of the TV camera. The iconoscope made good picture transmission possible.

PART I THE BEGINNING YEARS

No one invented television. Many researchers discovered how electricity works and how to transmit messages and sound. Thomas Edison, father of the electric light bulb, perfected the phonograph. Alexander Graham Bell developed the telephone. These inventions made TV possible.

As early as 1884, a German scientist named Paul Nipkow proposed the first practical TV. Television works by scanning. An exploring element criss-crosses or "scans" the image and generates a signal. At the receiving end the signal is reproduced as a picture. Nipkow developed a mechanical scanning disk. The picture was very poor, but mechanical disks were used until 1923. Then electronic scanning methods were discovered.

The most outstanding television developments were made by Vladimir Zworykin. He invented the first electronic camera tube, called an iconoscope. He also perfected the kinescope, the picture tube.

The first electronic TVs were crude, but modern television was born.

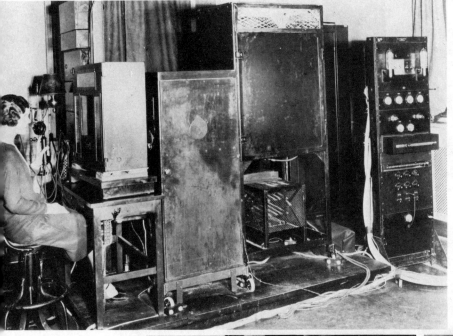

Left: the transmitting equipment used in the first intercity television demonstration. The model's face was scanned by a light beam that came through the opening in the cabinet. Photoelectric cells surrounded the opening. They picked up reflected light and transmitted it as an electrical signal. *Below left:* the back of an early TV receiver shows hundreds of wires. They connected the different segments to the neon-filled tubes. The current that passed through the wires created patterns of light and dark areas to form a picture.

Above right: the first TV drama was *The Queen's Messenger.* The sound was carried by the radio station WGY, and the picture was seen in four homes over an experimental station in upstate New York. The shots of the actress were primarily close-ups of her face.

THE BIRTH OF NBC AND CBS

By the mid 1920s researchers were working hard to improve television. E. F. W. Alexanderson of General Electric demonstrated the first home TV set in Schenectady, New York, in 1927. Meanwhile, radio boomed and the radio networks formed.

During World War I (1914–18), radio was vital to the Navy, which insisted on American ownership of the major radio company, the Marconi Wireless Company of America. It was taken over by the military, and after the war a new private company was formed, called the Radio Corporation of America (RCA).

RCA purchased WEAF (now WNBC) in New York from American Telephone and Telegraph (A.T.&T.). By 1926 RCA, Westinghouse, and General Electric together formed NBC (the National Broadcasting Company), the first radio network.

Later that year NBC bought another New York station, WJZ, and formed two networks. The Federal Communications Commission forced NBC to sell one network in 1943. It eventually became ABC (the American Broadcasting Company). RCA bought the shares of stock owned by Westinghouse and GE and became the sole owner of NBC.

The first television transmission by NBC was on October 30, 1931, on an experimental station in New York. The first TV "network" broadcast, in 1940, linked New York City with Schenectady.

CBS began in 1927 as United Independent Broadcasters, a radio network. The company was losing money and took in a partner, the Columbia Phonograph and Records Company, which withdrew from the partnership when the company continued to lose money.

Finally a young man named William S. Paley bought control of the network for $400,000 in 1928. Paley headed the network, renamed the Columbia Broadcasting System (CBS), until 1977.

From the 1940s until 1976, CBS led in the ratings. The A. C. Nielsen Company uses audience-counting devices to survey what programs the public watches. These devices are placed in 1,200 specially selected houses. Based on what these families watch, the Nielsen Company estimates the number of people who watch each TV program.

During the late 1970s ABC stunned the television industry by its rise to the top with action-packed programs and mini-series. ABC was long the number-one network for sports coverage.

FROM NEW YORK TO PHILLY

The stock market crash in 1929 slowed down experimentation with television.

The big event of the 1930s occurred when A.T.&T. and the Philadelphia Electric Storage Battery Company (Philco), a leading manufacturer of TV sets, laid a coaxial cable between New York and Philadelphia. A coaxial cable is heavily shielded wire that transmits signals. By the 1940s television programs were broadcast over cables, and the networks grew quickly.

In the United States the public "owns" the air waves. As television grew, there were conflicting claims to the air waves, so Congress created the Federal Communications Commission in 1934. The members of the FCC decide who uses TV channels, assign frequencies, and give licenses.

A rapid series of TV "firsts" occurred during the 1930s: the first musical comedy, the first boxing match, the first one-hour production, the first baseball game, and the first feature film were aired.

The studios were small and hot, and performers received small salaries—but TV programming was just beginning.

Here's the way Felix the Cat looked on the screens of experimental black-and-white television sets in the late 1920s. The picture was transmitted by RCA-NBC cameras from a studio in Manhattan all the way to Kansas.

Roy Rogers teamed up with his real-life wife Dale Evans for his TV show. While she sometimes helped him catch the villains, more often she had to be rescued by him.

PART II THE '40S: TV BOOMS

During the early 1940s the world was already torn by World War II. When the United States entered the war, television was all but forgotten. Factories were needed to make weapons, not television sets.

Few people owned TV sets before the war. Most Americans missed the first telecasts of an opera, a circus performance, a basketball game, even the first commercial.

When the war ended, television boomed. By the end of the 1940s, TV was in 34 million homes.

Television became a fierce competitor of radio. Big-name radio stars cautiously moved into TV. The types of programs we still watch came to television— comedies, westerns, news shows, cops and robbers programs, drama, and variety shows.

NBC sold one of its networks in 1943. Ten years later it became ABC, the third major network. The Emmy Awards, which are given to outstanding shows and performers by the members of the National Academy of Television Arts and Sciences, began in 1949.

Left: the Lone Ranger never shot to kill. He carried a silver bullet to remind himself to shoot only when absolutely necessary. His white horse was named Silver, and he was aided by Tonto, an expert scout. At the end of each show someone always asked, "Who was that masked man?" *Right:* aided by his horse Champion, Gene Autry captured the "bad guys" between songs on *The Gene Autry Show.*

WHO WAS
THAT MASKED MAN?

The Gene Autry Show, the first television western, galloped onto the screen in 1947 and spurred a flood of other westerns. Unlike westerns of today, the show featured more songs than gunfights. During the 1930s Gene Autry was the only cowboy in the box-office top ten.

In 1940 Autry moved into radio. His show, *Melody Ranch,* was aired for eighteen years. He was one of the first well-known stars to make special TV movies. When he wasn't singing "Back in the Saddle Again," he captured daring desperadoes.

Roy Rogers was the only other singing cowboy who became a TV star. *The Roy Rogers Show* (1951–56) mixed comedy and songs with action. Rogers and his wife, Dale Evans, ran the Double R Ranch. They often rescued their foolish cowhand, Pat Brady, especially when his jeep, Nellibell, acted up. Trigger, Roy's horse, was far more reliable than the temperamental jeep.

Roy Rogers rarely shot anyone. Adults accused him of turning westerns into "horse operas," but children loved him. Off-screen and on-screen, he was portrayed as a family man. He signed off with the song "Happy Trails to You."

Hopalong Cassidy was another cowboy who moved from films to television. He was the creation of a New York City worker, who wanted the character to limp, thus the name "Hopalong." But actor William Boyd got rid of the sore foot after the first film.

When Hopalong wasn't chasing cattle rustlers, he was the foreman of the Bar 20 Ranch. A young sidekick named Lucky shared his adventures. Another sidekick, played by Gabby Hayes, was a talkative old-timer who made everyone laugh.

The Lone Ranger overshadowed the other westerns of the decade because it was more dramatic. The Lone Ranger and Tonto, his Indian friend, "led the fight for law and order in the early West" (just as the narrator promised). He and Tonto captured bank robbers, cleared innocent men, broke up dangerous gangs, prevented stage-coach holdups, and stopped runaway wagons. Tonto called him "Kemo Sabe," which means "faithful friend."

The program was on network TV for twelve years before it was sold to non-network stations. It is the only early TV western still being rerun.

STICK 'EM UP!

Like westerns, crime programs moved from radio to prime-time television. The first private eye show was *Martin Kane, Private Eye*. Kane was a tough, determined New York City detective. Begun in 1949, the program had a five-year run and four leading men as Kane: Lee Tracy, Lloyd Nolan, William Gargan, and Mark Stevens.

Ralph Bellamy starred as Mike Barnett in the early detective series *Man Against Crime* (1949–53). Barnett was an unarmed private eye in New York. In each episode he searched for a clue. A signal told him how long to search in order to time the show, which was live.

Ellery Queen was a popular program. The character Ellery Queen was a writer and amateur detective, who first appeared in stories written by Frederic Dannay and the late Manfred B. Lee. Ellery was played by Lee Bowman, followed by Hugh Marlowe. Ellery's trademark was telling the audience the clue and then inviting the viewers to solve the mystery. He always named the guilty party after a commercial break and after he had gathered all the suspects in one room.

Ellery Queen was aired from 1950 to 1955. It was revived as *The Further Adventures of Ellery Queen* in 1958, but it only lasted one year. Even then, it did not disappear for good. It was temporarily revived in 1975.

Left: Mike Barnett (Ralph Bellamy) was often menaced, but there was little violence on *Man Against Crime*. There wasn't room on the small stage for pitched battles! Like all detectives, Barnett was sometimes involved in romantic encounters. Here, he's involved with Shirley Stoudley. *Right:* George Nader (*center*) was one of four men who played the role of *Ellery Queen* during the 1950s. Ellery was a clever amateur detective, and is seen here with Jeanne Moody and Scott Forbes.

Above: Sid Ceasar often played the shabby Professor, an "expert" on everything. As archeologist Professor Ludwig von Fossill, he advised, "Don't lift heavy rocks." Imogene Coca is listening to one of his wacky ideas.
Right: Milton Berle became known for his catchphrase, "I'll tell ya what I'm gonna do."

Mystery shows were so popular in the late 1940s and early 1950s that CBS broadcast three live mystery series each week. The programs were known in the industry as "The Weird Sisters." They were *Suspense* (1949), *Danger,* and *The Web* (both 1950). Several of today's movie stars appeared in *The Web,* notably Paul Newman, Jack Lemmon, and Lee Marvin.

MR. TELEVISION

Milton Berle was the first real TV star. His popular, noisy comedy show earned him the title "Mr. Television." Originally called the *Texaco Star Theater,* the show ran for eight years and changed its title and sponsor several times. Berle was so popular that in 1951 NBC gave him a contract for thirty years. He will be paid until 1981 even though he is not on the air.

Your Show of Shows, originally called *Admiral Broadway Review*, is a comedy classic. Sid Caesar and Imogene Coca starred. Following the signature song, "Stars Over Broadway," Caesar nervously introduced the guest star. His nervous cough became almost a trademark. Then ninety minutes of sophisticated comedy, top-notch singing, and pantomime held the audience spellbound.

Every seven days a complete "show of shows" was written, rehearsed, and performed, for in the 1940s all TV was live. Max Liebman was the director and producer. *Your Show of Shows* was the first variety show to have both a permanent cast and permanent writers.

Coca and Caesar created several comic characters. The two most famous ones were Charles and Doris Hickenlooper, a married couple with different ideas on everything. As a weekly feature, Caesar and his company mocked the movies. Their skits are unique in TV history.

Caesar and Coca were split up by NBC. From 1954 to 1957 Caesar starred in *Caesar's Hour,* which received good ratings. Nanette Fabray, Janet Blair, and Gisele MacKenzie played his wives. Coca's next show, *Grindle* (1963), was not popular and she returned to the theater.

For millions, Sunday night was "Ed Sullivan night" from 1948 to 1971. Ed Sullivan was the emcee for *The Toast of the Town,* later renamed *The Ed Sullivan Show.* The success of this long-running variety series was a puzzle. Sullivan's nervous mannerisms, stiff neck, and poor speech made him an unlikely host. His weekly promise of a "r-r-e-e-e-e-a-a-a-l-l-l-l-l-l-y-y-y-y-y big shew" was mimicked from coast to coast.

But he delivered his promise. He put together terrific shows with animal and circus acts, singers, dancers, and comics. He featured new performers such as the Beatles and often booked performers when they were controversial. His special mix of acts kept viewers tuned in for twenty-three years.

Arthur Godfrey also hosted variety programs. He began with *Arthur Godfrey's Talent Scouts* in 1948. Young professional performers competed, and an applause meter determined who won.

Later he hosted *Arthur Godfrey and His Friends,* an hour-long variety show. The regulars included LuAnn Sims, the McGuire Sisters, Pat Boone, and Julius LaRosa, whom Godfrey fired on the air.

ROBOT SPELLED BACKWARDS IS TOBOR

". . . operating from his secret mountain headquarters on the planet Earth, Captain Video rallies men of goodwill and leads them against the forces of evil everywhere! As he rockets from planet to planet,

Left: rock star Elvis Presley made his first TV appearance on *The Ed Sullivan Show.* At the time, his provocative swinging hips created quite a controversy. He was paid $50,000 for the performance. *Below:* Arthur Godfrey conducted radio and TV shows at the same time. On the air he was easy going, folksy, and witty. Advertisers loved to have him plug their products. He chuckled, "Howa'ya. Howa'ya."

Above: Captain Video was the hero of the day. A courageous fighter and scientific genius, he was aided by incredible equipment and gadgets. For one year he was played by Richard Coogan, who was replaced by Al Hodge. *Captain Video and His Video Rangers* was on the air from 1949 to 1956. *Left:* on *Space Patrol* the crew, led by Commander Corry, battled injustice in space and in every time era. The program was done live, and once a performer walked into a "stone wall" and knocked the set over in front of thousands of home viewers.

let's follow the champion of justice, truth, and freedom . . ." This announcement opened each episode of *Captain Video and His Video Rangers.*

The Captain and his crew traveled in their spaceship, *Galaxy;* they met and fought evil creatures throughout the universe in the 22nd century. Captain Video's worst enemy was Dr. Pauli, played by Hal Conklin. Viewers loved to hate him. Dr. Pauli was killed four times, but each time the children demanded his return. Once he was blown to bits and Captain Video had to invent a way to reassemble his atoms.

Tobor, another adversary, was a giant robot made of indestructible metal. His hands were great hooks, and he was controlled by the voice of his master, an evil woman named Atar. He was also killed off, but the fans demanded his return.

Surprisingly, the budget for this science fiction program was very low. The space helmets were little more than football helmets with goggles attached.

Captain Midnight was a rival science fiction, or "sci-fi," show. Like Captain Video, Captain Midnight fought evil forces everywhere. At the end of the program he gave a clue to the next week's adventure. The message was deciphered with the Secret Decoder Badge —which you could buy by sending in 25 cents and the foil seal from Ovaltine, a milk flavoring.

The best sci-fi show on the air was *Tom Corbett, Space Cadet.* The scripts were good and so were the special effects. What's amazing is that the show was done live.

Tom Corbett was a Solar Guard assigned to the *Rocket Polaris.* The other crew members were Astro, a Venusian navigator, Captain Strong, and the radar controller Roger Manning, who frequently yelled, "Aww, go blow your jets." When the show ended in the mid 1950s, thousands of children were disappointed.

Space Patrol was shown on Saturday mornings. Buzz Corry, played by Ed Kemmer, was the commander of Terra I. Like Captain Video, Commander Corry fought a mechanical villain; his name was Five. He, too, was controlled by a woman. Corry's sidekick, Cadet Happy, often exclaimed, "Smokin' rockets, Commander."

Sci-fi never lost its appeal. We still watch it intently.

SAY, KIDS,
WHAT TIME IS IT?

"It's Howdy Doody time!" roared the Peanut Gallery, the children on the set for the show. Children waited years to get tickets for *The Howdy Doody Show.*

Buffalo Bob Smith was a puppeteer and ventriloquist. He built the lively, noisy show around the 27-inch (68.5-cm) marionette Howdy Doody and Clarabell, a clown. The plot of the programs revolved around the conflict between Howdy, who wanted his circus to perform in town, and the mayor, Phineas T. Bluster, who objected to it.

The origin of *The Howdy Doody Show* was the radio program *Triple B Ranch.* A pilot TV program was produced and NBC loved it. *The Howdy Doody Show* premiered on December 27, 1947. The Howdy puppet wasn't even finished! Buffalo Bob said Howdy Doody was too shy to come out.

Clarabell the clown frequently stole the show. The Peanut Gallery screamed and yelled each time Clarabell sneaked up behind Buffalo Bob and shot seltzer water in his face.

Clarabell honked a horn to answer Yes or No. He only spoke once. On September 30, 1960, on the 2,343rd show, he said, "Good-bye, kids."

Puppet programs are always popular. Kukla and Ollie were two puppets that captured the hearts of children. They first appeared in a local show in Chicago in 1947. Then their creator, Burr Tillstrom, invited a woman, Fran Allison, to join them. The show became *Kukla, Fran, and Ollie.* In 1949 it became the first show ever seen from coast to coast.

Throughout the 1950s puppet shows continued to be popular. Ventriloquist Shari Lewis hosted several children's shows. She told stories, sang songs, and performed sketches. Her two most popular puppets were Lamb Chop and Charlie Horse.

Puppets, now updated as muppets, amuse children to this day.

Left: Kukla is the bald, gnome-like character. Ollie is the one-toothed dragon. Between them is their creator, Burr Tillstrom. Fran Allison chatted with the puppets, told stories, and sang. *Below:* ventriloquist Buffalo Bob and the puppet Howdy Doody were the stars of the enormously popular *Howdy Doody Show*, which lasted thirteen years.

PART III
THE '50S:
THE GOLDEN AGE
OF TELEVISION

The 1950s are called the Golden Age of Television because more stars, more new programs, and more top-notch dramas filled the screen than ever before or since. In addition, color was introduced to TV.

A Ford Foundation grant established the National Education Television System as an alternative to commercial television.

Television changed dramatically at the end of the decade, when videotape was perfected. A taped program can be stored and played at any time. Stars no longer needed to fear live TV and more of them agreed to appear on the TV screen.

Live dramas, costly and difficult to produce, were replaced primarily by situation comedies and westerns as the 1950s ended.

**Charlton Heston and Felicia Montealegre starred in the
TV dramatization of the classic book *Of Human Bondage*
by Somerset Maugham, presented by *Studio One*.**

A CORPSE WALKS

The 1950s are labeled the Golden Age of Television mainly because excellent dramas were aired almost nightly. Begun in the late 1940s, *Kraft Television Theatre, Ford Television Theatre,* and *Playhouse 90* continued in the 1950s. Nearly 30 dramatic shows premiered: *Front Row, Revlon Theatre, Fireside Theatre, Motorola Television Hour, Lux Video Theatre, Elgin Hour, Alcoa Theatre, Kaiser Aluminum Hour, Four Star Jubilee,* and others. Large companies jumped on the bandwagon to sponsor programs.

Kraft Foods was the first company to sponsor an hour-long drama. Approximately 650 plays were presented on *Kraft Television Theatre* in its eleven-year run (1949–1960). Novels, plays, and books were adapted for TV. Unknown writers were also given a chance to write for the TV screen.

Playhouse 90 was the most ambitious of the weekly dramas. It provided unforgettable plays such as *Requiem for a Heavyweight* (1956), *The Miracle Worker, Judgment at Nuremberg,* and *The Days of Wine and Roses.* All were made into movies. All are classics.

Robert Montgomery hosted the *Lucky Strike Theater* and sometimes starred as well. *The Hunchback of Notre Dame, Great Expectations, David Copperfield,* and other classics were presented. Highly talented actors and actresses performed.

Studio One presented classics such as Shakespeare's *Macbeth* and *Julius Caesar.* Westinghouse sponsored *Studio One.*

Hallmark Greeting Cards sponsored plays, specials, and operas. Among its presentations were *Peter Pan, Alice in Wonderland, Johnny Belinda, Arsenic and Old Lace, Saint Joan,* and *Pinocchio.* Wonderful Broadway and Hollywood performers starred under Hallmark's banner. Among them were Julie Harris, Elizabeth Ashley, George C. Scott, David McCallum, Tony Randall, and John Forsythe. Hallmark still sponsors ninety-minute specials.

The Petrified Forest starred Henry Fonda, Lauren Bacall, and Humphrey Bogart in his only TV role. It was aired on *Producers*

Showcase, as was *Our Town.* Frank Sinatra, Paul Newman, and Eva Marie Saint had the leading roles. Sinatra sang "Love and Marriage," the first hit song of TV.

The list of movie and theater stars who acted in TV dramas is very long. Virtually all the shows employed rising young talents: Andy Griffith, Cloris Leachman, Steve McQueen, Joanne Woodward, Grace Kelly, Cliff Robertson, and Sidney Poitier. Stars such as Spencer Tracy and Helen Hayes brought their talent to TV.

What's amazing is that they worked under very hot, bright lights for small salaries. All the shows were live; there were no "idiot cards." When a performer "went up on his lines" (forgot them), millions watched the stumbling. Cameras sometimes focused on the wrong person. Once a "corpse" got up and walked away.

But live television was a challenge. *The Kraft Television Theatre* once staged *A Night to Remember,* a drama of the sinking of the ship *Titanic.* There were 107 actors, 31 sets, and seven cameras—all on a small TV stage.

The high costs and technical difficulties eventually led to the death of live drama. As the 1950s ended, the dramatic programs were replaced by westerns and situation comedies, known today as "sit-coms."

HI YA, MISS KITTY

The first TV westerns were for children. The adult western hit the screen with the premiere of *Cheyenne.* Clint Walker starred as a frontier scout. The success of *Cheyenne* caused a stampede of TV westerns.

Gunsmoke was enormously popular. It lasted for twenty years. James Arness played Marshall Matt Dillon of Dodge City for the entire run. *Gunsmoke* was not always a traditional western. Dillon made mistakes; he once hung the wrong man. He was occasionally out-

Doc Adams (Milburn Stone), deputy Chester Goode (Dennis Weaver),
Kitty Russell (Amanda Blake) and Marshal Matt Dillon (James Arness)
were the best of friends on *Gunsmoke.* For 20 years this
classic western was a Saturday night staple. Begun as a
30-minute program, it was expanded to 60 minutes in 1961.

Left: Richard Boone starred as Paladin, a professional gunslinger. He smoked fifty-eight-cent cigars, quoted poetry, and collected chessmen. His business card read "Have Gun, Will Travel Wire Paladin, Hotel Carlton, San Francisco." *Above:* on *Bonanza* there was actually very little gunplay, but a lot of fatherly advice. The critics called it a soap opera set in the West. Lorne Greene played the widowed father. His sons were played by Dan Blocker (Hoss), Michael Landon (Little Joe), and Pernell Roberts (Adam).

drawn or shot from undercover without warning. As the years went by, TV critics complained about violence and Dillon shot less and talked more.

The number of westerns grew. Each featured a unique hero. Paladin was the hero of *Have Gun, Will Travel.* He was well educated and worldly.

James Garner starred as the cowardly hero Bret Maverick. He was slow on the draw. He disliked horses and the outdoors. And he wasn't honest. *Maverick* was a spoof, but a lot of viewers took it seriously. Garner was perfect for the role, and he became a star. He's currently the gun-shy detective on *The Rockford Files.*

Bonanza galloped off with top ratings for most of the 1960s. The plots concerned the problems and adventures of the Cartwrights, who owned the huge Ponderosa ranch.

Rawhide was built around the adventures of two men who drove cattle from Texas to Kansas. Eric Fleming and Clint Eastwood starred. Begun in 1959, *Rawhide* lasted until 1965 and made Eastwood a star.

The Virginian (1962–70) was the first ninety-minute western. The original cast included Doug McClure, James Drury (the Virginian), Lee J. Cobb, and Roberta Shore.

TV "oaters" (fans of westerns) were watching thirty-two adult westerns each week during prime time in 1959. Westerns declined during the 1960s and are almost nonexistent today except for reruns.

Like westerns, police programs provided plenty of shooting. *The Untouchables* is considered one of the most violent shows ever aired. Robert Stack starred as Eliot Ness, a leader of an elite group of government law enforcers. Set during the Prohibition Era when liquor was illegal, there were a lot of hijacked beer trucks and machine-gun battles with organized crime hoodlums.

In *Highway Patrol,* Broderick Crawford as Dan Matthews, patrol chief, barked "ten-four" into his squad car radio. Chases, generally by car but sometimes by helicopter, were a part of most plots. *Highway Patrol* paved the way for similar police programs.

Dragnet was notable for its realism. Jack Webb played Detective Sergeant Joe Friday, a calm, unemotional cop. He invariably told the witnesses, "All we want are the facts, ma'am." His partner was Detective Frank Smith (Ben Alexander). The series was revived in 1969 with Jack Webb and Harry Morgan in the leads.

GOOD NIGHT, GRACIE, AND GOOD NIGHT, MRS. CALABASH

During the early 1950s the popular radio and vaudeville comedians flocked to television. The enormous appetite for new jokes and new gags eventually swallowed up the comedy shows. By the 1960s there were few comedy variety shows. The best comics were now "guests" or sit-com stars.

Jack Benny had a TV show while he was still on the radio. For years and years he claimed he was thirty-nine. His age and his cheapness were the targets of many jokes. When a holdup man said, "Your money or your life," Jack paused. The robber yelled, "Hurry up." Jack replied, "I'm thinking it over."

Bob Hope is another TV immortal. He began his career in vaudeville. In 1952 his monthly TV show was born. He always did a monologue of jokes about politics, current events or popular personalities. His smooth, easy delivery and perfect timing make him one of America's best loved comics. He is considered to be the best "host" on TV and he repeatedly hosts the Academy Awards.

Red Skelton was a Tuesday night staple from 1953 to 1970. A top mime and clown, he created dozens of characters such as Clem Kaddidlehopper, a country bumpkin; and Freddie the Freeloader, a tramp.

Beady-eyed Jimmy Durante appeared on *The Four Star Revue, The All-Star Revue, The Colgate Comedy Hour,* and *The Texaco Star Theatre* in the early 1950s. He sang, danced, played the piano, and stamped his feet to his theme song, "Ink-a-Dink-a-Doo." He ended each show with the words, "Good night Mrs. Calabash."

Left: George Burns and the late Gracie Allen were television's best loved comedy couple. They played themselves in a sit-com. George was the straight man, and Gracie was his addle-brained wife. He'd come downstage and predict the outcome of her problem between puffs on his cigar. When Gracie gave her dizzy explanations, he'd tell her "Say good night, Gracie." She always replied, "Good night, Gracie." *Below left:* Bob Hope travels the globe entertaining America's troops, especially at Christmastime. In the 1950s he visited Korea, and in 1968 he visited the Armed Forces in Vietnam. His tours were broadcast as specials. *Below right:* Mel Blanc does one of his most famous characterizations as Professor Le Blanc. Here he gives violin lessons to Jack Benny, whose screechy, out-of-tune playing was a running joke.

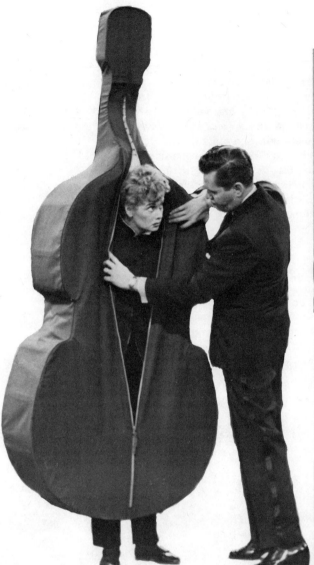

Left: on the *I Love Lucy* show, Lucille Ball played a housewife who longed for a career in show business. She tried almost anything to get into her husband's nightclub act. *Above:* Vivian Vance, who played Lucy's wacky friend on *I Love Lucy*, also co-starred on *The Lucy Show* (1967–68). On both programs the two women continually schemed to raise money or outwit the men in their lives.

Right: the comic interplay between Jackie Gleason as Ralph and Art Carney as sewer worker Ed Norton made *The Honeymooners* a classic. Ralph constantly complained about his work as a bus driver and looked for schemes to get rich.

TO THE MOON, ALICE

Two comedy shows stand out above all the rest in TV history—*I Love Lucy* and *The Honeymooners*. Lucille Ball as Lucy was a loving but wacky wife. Desi Arnaz was her TV husband and at that time her real-life husband. He played the role of a hot-blooded Cuban bandleader named Ricky Ricardo.

Lucy's silly plans always got her into trouble. She was aided in her schemes by Ethel Mertz (Vivian Vance). The plots frequently revolved around her lame-brain schemes to perform with Ricky's band Together with Fred Mertz (William Frawley), Ricky found ways to make Lucy's plans backfire. Lucille Ball was an excellent slapstick comedienne. *I Love Lucy* was first aired in 1951. It was an immediate hit and remained a top-rated show for years. It is still rerun on local stations.

In 1957 Lucy and Desi switched to a monthly comedy hour, *The Lucille Ball–Desi Arnaz Show.* The series ended with their divorce three years later.

The Honeymooners began as a skit on *The Jackie Gleason Show,* a comedy variety hour. Jackie Gleason developed a number of comic characters, the most popular of which was Ralph Kramden. He became the central character of *The Honeymooners.*

Ralph was a bus driver and one half of the honeymooners. The other half was Alice, played by Audrey Meadows. They lived in a flat in Brooklyn. Ralph got into all kinds of jams, and his wife got him out. When Alice rejected his insane ideas, he'd roar, "To the moon, Alice, to the moon." But by the end of the thirty minute show, he'd say, "Baby, you're the greatest."

Amos 'n' Andy dealt with the comic misadventures of two blacks who were buddies. They ran the Fresh Air Taxi Company on the south side of Chicago.

Amos 'n' Andy was one of the most popular radio programs of all time. The move from radio to TV was predictable. A third char-

(33)

acter was added named Kingfish (Tim Moore), who dreamed up ridiculous ways to swindle hard-working Andy.

Audiences loved the program and laughed each time Amos said, "Holy mackerel, there Andy." But its production ended in 1953, when organizations such as the NAACP objected to its demeaning image of blacks.

The only black roles on TV, except for the characters on *Amos 'n' Andy,* were minor ones. Blacks usually worked as menial laborers or domestic servants such as the women on *Beulah.* Occasionally black singers and dancers appeared on variety shows.

Bud Abbott and Lou Costello were another troublesome pair. They first appeared on *The Colgate Comedy Hour* and later created mischief on the *Abbott and Costello Show.* Their "Who's on first?" routine is famous. On reruns of their series Costello is heard yelling, "Hey, A-b-b-bott."

WHAT A REVOLTIN' DEVELOPMENT THIS IS

Family situation comedies came to TV during the 1940s and quickly multiplied. *Life With Luigi, The Goldbergs,* and *Mama* were sentimental family comedies with an ethnic touch.

The majority of the series centered on the father. In 1949 Jackie Gleason, not yet a star, played Chester Riley in *The Life of Riley.* It only lasted a year.

The show returned to TV in 1953 with William Bendix as the star and became a hit. Bendix was ideal for the role of a hardworking but bumbling father. He and his pal Gillis worked as riveters for an aircraft company. Riley was gullible and Gillis often tricked him.

On the radio program *Father Knows Best* the father did not know best. He was a typical bumbling father. But on TV he was calm and intelligent.

Jane Wyatt and Robert Young played the parents on *Father Knows Best*. Father's advice helped his three children, Bud (Billy Gray), Cathy (Laurin Chapin), and Betty (Elinor Donahue) solve all their problems.

Left: Superman (George Reeves) repeatedly saved his friend
Lois Lane (Noel Neill) by using his X-ray vision, super-hearing,
super-breath, and super-strength. There was no mistaking
Superman. He dressed in a blue costume, red boots, and a
yellow belt with a gold buckle. *Right:* a favorite of children,
Lassie premiered in 1954. A beautiful Collie, she saved her
masters and others from all types of disasters. No animal
series captured the hearts of children as *Lassie* did.

The real-life Nelson family starred in *The Adventures of Ozzie and Harriet* (1952–1966). The comedy centered around their sons, Ricky and David, in common situations. Dad was always around to give advice. As the family got older, the series changed to include the wives of David and Ricky. This was the first successful sit-com on ABC.

Danny Thomas in *Make Room for Daddy* encountered humorous problems, generally about his job as a nightclub comedian. The show was renamed *The Danny Thomas Show,* when Jean Hagan, who played his wife, left the program. Danny became a widower, but within a year he remarried.

Later, Danny Thomas starred in *Make Room for Granddaddy,* but it only lasted a year.

The troubles families face on TV became more dramatic and more important over the years, but the basic format is the same. The family always sticks together to lick the problem.

LOOK, UP IN THE SKY!

Superman, able to leap tall buildings in a single bound, leaped from the comics and radio to television in 1951. A "strange visitor" from the planet Krypton, Superman was disguised as a mild-mannered reporter named Clark Kent. He worked for a newspaper named *The Daily Planet.*

George Reeves played the dual role of Clark Kent and Superman. A lot of the suspense revolved around Kent's methods of changing into Superman. He frequently shed his suit and glasses in a telephone booth or closet.

Superman comics are still sold. The character Superman was originally created by two teen-agers, Jerry Siegel and Joseph Shuster—though they were in their twenties before they found a publisher.

During the 1950s children were offered all kinds of programs. A popular show was *Winky Dink and You.* Winky Dink was an animated elflike character who was always finding himself in tight spots. With their Winky Dink kits the children watching drew countless bridges and ladders, which Winky used to escape. The kit contained a sheet of plastic that was placed on the TV screen and crayons that wiped off. Jack Barry gave the drawing instructions.

The first Hollywood studio to enter the TV field was Walt Disney Productions. The program *Disneyland* provided something different each week—cartoons, nature films, or action and adventure stories. The most popular story was about Davy Crockett, a frontier scout. The song "The Ballad of Davy Crockett" was number one on the Hit Parade for weeks. Every kid on the block sported a fake coonskin hat.

Animal stars were loved by children. *Lassie,* a dog, is the best-known animal heroine to this day.

SPECTACULAR! DAZZLING! DON'T MISS IT!

Sylvester ("Pat") Weaver, a president of NBC, planned the first specials. He called them "spectaculars." During the 1950s, no one interrupted the regular TV schedule, and his idea for one-time shows was unusual.

The first spectacular was *Satins and Spurs,* a ninety-minute western musical comedy, starring Betty Hutton. The critics and the audience disliked it, but specials still took hold.

Some specials were yearly events, especially the Christmas programs. *Amahl and the Night Visitors,* an opera story of the birth of Christ, was first commissioned for TV in 1951. *Amahl and the Night Visitors* was the first sponsored network show in color.

The special *Peter Pan* was a great success. J. M. Barrie's classic

Top: Mary Martin was a sensation as *Peter Pan.* The songs "I'm Flying" and "Never Smile at a Crocodile" from the show were big hits in 1955. *Bottom: Amahl and the Night Visitors* is a classic opera aired annually during the Christmas season. It is the story of a crippled 12-year-old boy and the three kings. Left to right are Willis Patterson, Richard Cross, John McCollum, and Kurt Yaghjian.

Left: the late Bing Crosby starred in his own show. Though his records sold millions, he did not reach the top of the ratings. He did a sit-com, *The Bing Crosby Show,* emceed the *Hollywood Palace,* hosted the *Bing Crosby Golf Tournament,* and sang on numerous specials, which were generally well-liked. *Center:* Pat Boone was a regular on *Arthur Godfrey's Talent Scouts* before he had his own show during the 1950s. He later starred in Hollywood movies and made special guest appearances on TV. As a young man, Boone's trademark was his white buck shoes. He conveyed a wholesome image. *Right:* Perry Como shed his traditional cardigan sweater for formal wear to appear on a TV special.

play is about a boy (played, in fact, by Mary Martin) who doesn't want to grow up. He convinces Wendy, Michael, and John to go with him to Never Never Land. There they battle with Captain Hook (played on TV by Cyril Ritchard).

For three years *Peter Pan* was produced live. When videotape was perfected, it was aired yearly until 1976, when a new version was done. Mia Farrow starred, but she received much less attention and praise as Peter Pan than had Mary Martin. The success of *Peter Pan* spurred the production of other fairy tales, such as *Aladdin* and *Cinderella.*

Actually, specials had been presented prior to *Satins and Spurs,* but they were not called "specials." The first real special was the two-hour *Ford's 50th Anniversary Show,* which was telecast by both NBC and CBS in 1953. A number of stars performed, but Mary Martin and Ethel Merman stopped the show with their duet of songs.

Today a great number of specials are musicals, but some successful dramatic series, such as *The Waltons,* began as specials. Sporting events are often aired as specials, too.

THE SOUNDS OF MUSIC

Singers tested their vocal chords on TV, but often the most successful recording stars failed on the screen.

Perry Como was the first popular singer on TV. He sang in a relaxed style on *The Chesterfield Supper Club* on NBC in 1948. The show was fifteen minutes long. *The Perry Como Show* on CBS was aired next; it was eventually expanded to an hour. It became the top-rated Saturday night program. In 1963 Perry Como decided to give up the weekly grind in favor of specials.

Dinah Shore was the only female singer to achieve a huge success with a weekly series. Her show alternated with Perry Como's. In the mid 1950s she began an hour-long program. The musical numbers on *The Dinah Shore Chevy Show* were brilliant. The popularity of musical variety shows waned in the 1960s, and Dinah Shore appeared only on specials. During the 1970s she hosted a talk show. Her warm, folksy manner made *Dinah's Place* a success.

Frank Sinatra's records sold by the millions, but he tried a weekly series from 1950 to 1952 and again in 1957 and 1958, and both failed. His specials, however, always attracted a large audience.

Like Sinatra, Judy Garland was a major star who never had a truly successful series on TV. During the 1950s a dispute with CBS caused her to walk out on her show. Finally in 1962 she appeared in a special that won rave reviews. The next year she launched a weekly series, but it was on at the same time as the western *Bonanza,* which trampled it in the ratings.

Andy Williams was introduced to TV audiences by Steve Allen in 1954. He became a summer replacement for Pat Boone and Garry Moore. During the 1960s he starred in his own weekly series. His relaxed, friendly singing won him a following. The Osmond Brothers sang regularly on his program. Donny Osmond and his sister Marie went on to star in a dazzling musical variety show on ABC during the 1970s.

SIGN IN, PLEASE

Phyllis McGinley once quipped, "On all the channels, nothing but panels." Because they are cheap to produce, panel shows filled the air waves. The father of them all was *What's My Line?* The panel members guessed the occupations of the contestants after they signed in. If the contestant stumped the panel, he or she won $50.

Several of today's game shows are flashier versions of old programs. The prizes are bigger and the panels are filled with stars. The first big-money quiz program was *The $64,000 Question,* which pre-

Above: What's My Line? celebrated its fifteenth anniversary on the air in 1965. Arlene Frances, Bennett Cerf, and Dorothy Kilgallen were the regular panelists. John Daly was the moderator. All appear here with guest star Ernie Kovacs. *Right:* Charles Van Doren, winner of $129,000 on the night-time quiz show *Twenty-One,* eventually told a House of Representatives committee that he received answers in advance. By then he was a celebrity and a summer replacement for David Garroway on the *Today Show.* The investigations prompted lawsuits by the losers, which were unsettled for years.

Dorothy (played by Judy Garland) had landed in a strange world.
Only the Wizard of Oz was capable of sending her back to Kansas.
Following the yellow brick road to the Wizard's castle, she met a
rusty tin man, a scarecrow without a brain, and a cowardly lion.

miered in 1955 during prime time. Emcee Hal March asked experts questions on the subjects they chose. A contestant doubled his or her winnings with each correct answer. Each week the questions became more difficult. TV audiences loved cheering the contestants on.

The enormous popularity of *The $64,000 Question* led to a spin-off, *The $64,000 Challenge.* Quiz shows such as *$100,000 Surprise, Twenty-One,* and *Dotto* followed.

Rumors spread that the shows were "fixed." A grand jury investigation revealed that the answers were sometimes given to contestants on *Twenty-One* and *Dotto.* The scandal shocked the public and ruined the image of all the quiz shows. Actually, faking questions was not, strictly speaking, illegal, but all the big-money shows went off the air.

FOLLOW THE YELLOW BRICK ROAD

The movie industry fought television at first. When it became evident that TV was winning, the studios decided to "join 'em." Movie studios could boost their earnings by selling movies to television. By the mid 1950s the major studios went a step further and began producing made-for-TV movies and series. In 1954 Walt Disney Productions was the first major studio to produce for television.

When CBS bought the TV rights to *The Wizard of Oz* from M-G-M, it was a major breakthrough. Starring Judy Garland, the film made its TV debut on November 3, 1956. Three years later it was shown again and it's been an annual event ever since.

The movie dam really burst in 1956 when RKO sold 740 movies to C&C Super Corporation, which leased them to TV. Now the other studios sold movies to TV, but only those made before 1948. After

1960 the studios sold their post-1948 movies. NBC started the flood of movies with *Saturday Night at the Movies*.

The success of the movies drove up the prices. By the 1970s the networks sought blockbusters. *Gone with the Wind* cost NBC $5,000,000 for a single showing and the commercials cost the advertisers $250,000 a minute. *Gone with the Wind* attracted more viewers than any other movie. NBC later paid a record $7,000,000 for *The Godfather*.

Today prime-time television is dominated by movies.

WHITER THAN WHITE

Soap operas, which dominate daytime television, are the continuing dramatic stories of two or more families. These families usually live in a small or medium-size town. The characters are confronted by death, divorce, murder, and less dramatic problems of daily life. Often they are doctors or lawyers. "The soaps" are so called because the majority of their sponsors were and are soap companies. They promise bold colors and "whiter than white" clothes. The first soaps were fifteen minutes long.

The first popular soap was *Search for Tomorrow*, begun in 1951. It's still going strong. The main character has always been Joanne Vincente, played by Mary Stuart. Over the years she's dealt with the death of her husbands and the troubles of her family and friends. The story is beginning to shift to the younger generations of the fictive town of Henderson.

As the World Turns is the dramatic story of the residents of Oakdale, primarily the Hughes and Stewart families. Launched in 1956, it was the first thirty-minute soap opera. It is consistently the number-one-rated soap.

The Edge of Night deals with ordinary people in difficult circumstances, with an emphasis on crime detection and courtroom scenes.

Left: Chris (Don MacLaughlin) and Nancy (Helen Wagner) as they appeared on *As the World Turns* in 1959. *Right:* Mary Stuart, Queen of the Soaps, stars as Joanne Vincente on *Search for Tomorrow.* She's been on the series since it began in 1951. With her is Joel Higgins, who plays Bruce Carson.

Below: Dr. Roger Coleridge (Ron Hale) is a wealthy bachelor, who is still involved with Delia Reid Ryan (Ilene Kristen), his ex-lover. They are key characters on *Ryan's Hope.*

Above left: Edward R. Murrow was a top-flight reporter whose greatest moment came in 1954 when he exposed the unfair tactics Senator Joseph McCarthy used to find supposed Communists. *Right:* the combination of a somber Huntley and a witty Brinkley made them a successful news team on the nightly news. *Below:* the effect of TV on politics was clear in 1952. Richard Nixon was Dwight D. Eisenhower's running mate for the presidential election but was charged with misusing campaign funds. He went on nationwide television to tell the voters he accepted only one gift as a politician, a black-and-white dog named Checkers. He told the audience that he intended to keep it.

Both *The Edge of Night* and *As the World Turns* are still sudsing, and they were both launched on the same day.

Throughout the 1960s and 1970s as one soap washed away, another rolled in. Premiered in 1965, *The Days of Our Lives* is centered on Dr. Thomas Horton, a professor of medicine at University Hospital, and his family. It was the first soap to include musical numbers.

Soap operas are shown every weekday, Monday through Friday, so they are part of the daily lives of their millions of viewers. The popularity of the soaps also led to a spoof called *Soap,* which began in 1977.

I INTEND TO KEEP CHECKERS

News coverage is a vital function of TV. The time allotted to the news greatly increased recently, especially if compared to the early 1950s, when the news programs were only fifteen minutes long. John Cameron Swayze (NBC) and Douglas Edwards (CBS) presented roundups of the nightly news. They gave brief reports, backed by film clips.

TV coverage of political campaigns revolutionized elections. The first political convention covered by TV was in 1948. The cameras were stationed outside the meeting halls. They were not allowed on the floor of the convention centers until 1952, the year the conventions became really big shows.

Chet Huntley and David Brinkley were teamed by NBC to cover the 1956 presidential conventions. They were a hit and they went on to do the *Huntley-Brinkley Report* on the nightly news.

Documentaries, or factual reports, were given a lot of air time during the 1950s. *See It Now* was the best documentary series. Edward R. Murrow was the moderator.

Newscasters traveled the globe. The public watched the investigations by the Senate's Kefauver Committee into organized crime; the crisis over the Suez Canal, when Egypt threatened to close it; and the arrival of federal troops in Little Rock, Arkansas, to enforce school integration. That was just the beginning. Throughout the 1960s and 1970s TV newsmen and camera crews would go everywhere.

YAKKITY-YAK

TV programming was originally scheduled for daytime and prime evening time. Before too long TV executives expanded the schedules to begin very early in the morning and end after midnight. Talk programs were slotted for these hours because they are cheap to produce.

Broadway Open House (1950–51) was the pioneer late-night show. Jerry Lester was the master of ceremonies. It was an informal talk show, with performers "dropping in."

The top late-night show is *The Tonight Show,* begun in 1954. Steve Allen and Jack Paar were the first hosts before Johnny Carson took over in 1962.

The talk show *Today* was introduced for early morning viewers in 1952. It combined news, music, and chitchat. The first host was Dave Garroway. He was often upstaged by an unusual cast member, a chimpanzee named J. Fred Muggs.

Over the years the *Today* show became more news-oriented and a number of hosts came and went: Hugh Downs, John Chancellor, Barbara Walters, and Frank McGee. Tom Brokaw and Jane Pauley are the current co-hosts.

Talk shows began to fill daytime and even prime-time hours. *The Mike Douglas Show* is a popular daily talk-variety program. Douglas is known for his pleasant interviews and conversation.

Above left: Barbara Walters left the *Today* show in 1976 to co-anchor the news on ABC. She reportedly received a contract for one million dollars a year. *Above right:* Johnny Carson's boyish charm keeps *The Tonight Show* popular. *Right:* Mike Douglas asks performers and well-known personalities to co-host his daily show. Superstar and director Burt Reynolds was a co-host for a week.

PART IV
THE '60S: THE VAST WASTELAND

The quality of TV programming peaked in the mid 1950s and then plunged downhill fast. In 1961 Newton N. Minow, the new chairman of the FCC, told the members of the National Association of Broadcasting, "When TV is good, nothing—not the theater, not the magazines, or newspapers, nothing—is better. But when TV is bad, nothing is worse." He said the networks all showed the same programs: game shows, westerns, silly comedies, violent shows, and commercials, commercials, commercials. He labeled TV a "vast wasteland." But for most Americans, watching TV was a habit.

The 1960s are remembered for more color, more movies, and more specials as the networks competed in the ratings game.

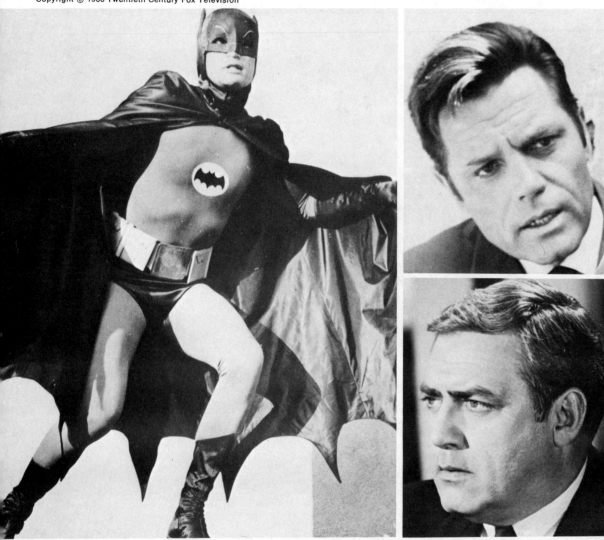

Left: Batman was played by Adam West. During his fights with the evil villains of Gotham City, the words POW and BAM were superimposed on the screen in comic-book style. Batman and Robin originally appeared in *Detective Comics* in 1939. *Bottom right:* Raymond Burr played the tough but "human" former detective Robert T. Ironside. A sniper's bullet left him paralyzed, but he continued to solve crimes as a police consultant. *Top right:* Jack Lord, as investigator Steve McGarrett on *Hawaii Five-O.*

ZAM!
WHAM!!
POW!!!

Batman was really Bruce Wayne, a master scientist. He adopted Dick Greyson, who became Robin. Batman's parents were killed by gangsters when he was fourteen, so he and Robin fought the villains of Gotham City such as Penguin and Catwoman. Batman and Robin were known as the Dynamic Duo. Batgirl, the daughter of the police commissioner, occasionally worked with them.

Unlike the original Batman of the comic books, who was a straight fantasy character, the *Batman* of TV was a spoof. It was intended for adult audiences, but it quickly became a children's favorite too. The program only lasted two years (1966–68), but the reruns are still on the air. *Batman* spurred the sale of super-hero figures and automobiles.

Super-heroes were the new TV idols of children. During the 1970s *The Six Million Dollar Man, The Bionic Woman,* and *Wonder Woman* were hits. Each used special powers to thwart criminals.

More realistic crime programs included *Ironside.* Though paralyzed by a bullet wound and confined to a wheelchair, Chief Robert T. Ironside (Raymond Burr) continues his work as a special consultant to the San Francisco Police Department.

Hawaii Five-O is a long-running, hard-hitting show. Jack Lord stars as police chief Steve McGarrett. The spectacular scenery of the city of Honolulu and Oahu island makes the program quite different from other police dramas.

Naked City was a realistic police series, which was a half-hour long in 1958. It was revived as an hour-long drama in 1960 and ran for three years. The plots were about ordinary people under pressure.

(55)

Adam-12 was a police series about the day-to-day events in the lives of two young patrol officers. Adam-12 was the code name for their car. It was a low-key drama starring Martin Milner and Kent McCord.

As always, private detectives fought crime on the TV screen. Mike Connors starred as *Mannix* (1967–1976), a tough private eye. He was shot at and chased weekly while his secretary held down the office.

PREPARE TO
BEAM DOWN

No sci-fi show captured the attention of the public more than *Star Trek*. Captain James Kirk (William Shatner) commanded the *U.S.S. Enterprise* spacecraft, which explored the frontiers of space. Spock (Leonard Nimoy) was the Science Officer. Half Earthling and half Vulcan, he was extremely logical and unemotional.

The crew encountered incredible creatures from outer space and raced other ships across the galaxies. They often "beamed down" to alien planets.

The history of *Star Trek* is unusual. It failed to attract a large mass audience during its three seasons on NBC (1966–69), but the reruns on local stations ran away with the ratings. In 1979, a movie version of *Star Trek* was produced.

Twilight Zone was a series of tales of the supernatural. These dramas were noted for their surprise endings and good performances. *Twilight Zone* won several Emmys and attracted thousands of faithful fans.

Following the amazing success of a movie entitled *Star Wars,* a new sci-fi program was introduced on TV in 1978—*Battlestar Galactica.* It was noted for its high-budget special effects, but failed to attract a large audience and was canceled after one season.

Right: Guy Williams and June Lockhart starred in *Lost in Space,* but it was the robot who often stole the show. From the first sci-fi adventures on TV, robots were frequently a part of the cast. *Below:* Captain Kirk (*right*) treats everyone as equals except during a crisis when he must give orders to ensure their safety. His romantic encounters with creatures from alien planets always end when duty calls. Spock's logical thinking often saved the crew; his pointy ears make him easy to recognize.

Left: each member of the Impossible Mission Force specialized in a skill needed to thwart their enemies. Greg Morris as Barney Collier was a specialist in explosives and electronics. Using a team of heroes was a popular way to integrate the casts during the '60s and to include women as heroines. *Center:* on *I Spy,* two American agents posed as a tennis player and his trainer. They traveled the globe to protect the United States. Bill Cosby was the first black performer to star in a dramatic series. Robert Culp played the other lead. *Right:* comedian Don Adams was ideal as the bumbling Agent 86 on *Get Smart.* His catchphrases were echoed by everyone. Each time he made a mistake (and he made a lot), he'd say, "Oops, sorry about that, chief." To explain his dumb encounters he'd ask, "Would you believe . . . ?"

OOPS, SORRY ABOUT THAT

Spy programs became popular because of the increased competition between Russia and the United States in the space race.

The Man from U.N.C.L.E. featured Robert Vaughn as agent Napoleon Solo and David McCallum as agent Illya Kuryakin. They fought against the sinister opponents from THRUSH, and they used unique scientific gadgets. The dry cleaning shop Del Florias was the secret headquarters for U.N.C.L.E., the United Network Command for Law Enforcement.

On *Mission: Impossible* Mr. Phelps (played by Peter Graves) received a tape each week giving him his assignment. The voice on the tape said, "As always, should you or any of your Impossible Mission Force be caught or killed, the Secretary will disavow any knowledge of your actions. This tape will self-destruct in five seconds. Good luck."

The hour-long episodes were built around complicated spy missions. Highly technical devices and brilliant disguises helped the Force make their entrances and escapes from foreign countries, embassies, and jails. The scenes were extremely tense and well played by the cast: Barbara Bain, Martin Landau, Greg Morris, Peter Graves, and Peter Lupus.

With spys spying on all the channels a spoof was inevitable. *Get Smart* starred Don Adams as Agent Maxwell Smart, also known as Agent 86. He bumbled all his assignments for C.O.N.T.R.O.L. His weapons, ridiculously disguised, never worked, but he somehow succeeded in his battles against K.A.O.S. Each time he made a mistake he said, "Oops, sorry about that, chief."

CAN THE CAMP

Screwball comedies were campy (very extreme) during the early 1960s.

The Munsters (1964–66) mocked horror films. A family of odd creatures tried to live ordinary lives. Herman (Fred Gwynne) was a Frankenstein lookalike; he was gentle and dumb. His wife (Yvonne DeCarlo) got him and his father out of trouble whenever they tried to invent a new recipe or gadget.

The Addams Family was about another spooky clan. The program, produced by Filmways, was based on the cartoons of Charles Addams.

Programs about country bumpkins flourished. The wackiest sit-com was *The Beverly Hillbillies.* The critics hated it, but it was an immediate hit. Basically, the hillbillies outwitted the city slickers every week.

Andy Griffith was a country bumpkin on his own show in which he played a small-town sheriff. His deputy was the inept Don Knotts as Barney. Highly popular, *The Andy Griffith Show* lasted eight years and spun off *Mayberry R.F.D.*

Fantasy sit-coms were popular. *Mister Ed,* a Filmways production, starred a talking horse named Mister Ed. The comedy revolved around the fact that no one but his owner heard him speak.

Military life came in for its share of ribbing in sit-coms such as *The Wackiest Ship in the Army, F Troop,* and *McHale's Navy.* Earlier *The Phil Silvers Show* centered on Sergeant Bilko, a con artist in the Army.

Gomer Pyle, USMC was a smash hit about a naive yokel in the U.S. Marine Corps. Jim Nabors as the marine drove his tough sergeant (played by Frank Sutton) insane with his antics and innocence.

These zany, far-fetched comedies are only a handful of the ones aired during the 1960s. They represented a new low in the opinion of the TV critics, but the public loved them. They did not en-

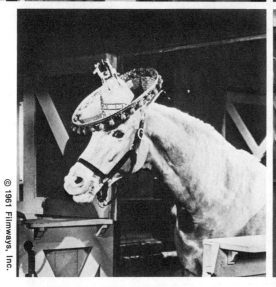

Top left: in *My Three Sons,* the oldest son Robbie (Don Grady) quarreled with his girlfriend while he was babysitting, so he took the baby home. Fred MacMurray is the father, Barry Livingston the youngest son, Ernie. *Top right:* the Addams family poses for a family portrait. Seated is Carolyn Jones as Morticia, flanked by Lisa Loring and Ken Weatherwax as the children. Standing on the left is Jackie Coogan as Uncle Fester, John Astin as Gomez Addams, Blossom Rock as Grandmama. *Bottom left:* Alan Young played the owner of the talking horse, Mister Ed. *Bottom right: Hogan's Heroes* was a far-out comedy of Allied soldiers in a German POW (Prisoner of War) camp. Hogan (Bob Crane) is in the first row on the left.

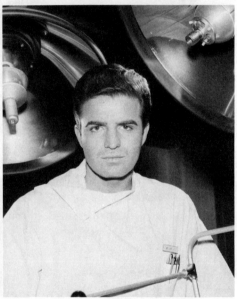

Left: to free his clients from jail, Perry Mason (Raymond Burr, right) sometimes called unusual witnesses to the stand. The investigative legwork was generally done by Paul Drake (William Hopper, left), a private eye. *Top right:* handsome Richard Chamberlain played the role of Dr. Kildare, an idealistic intern at Blair General Hospital, which Dr. Gillespie (Raymond Massey) headed. *Bottom right:* Ben Casey was the chief resident in neurosurgery at County General Hospital. He usually failed to button his tunic, but was very skilled and dedicated. Dark, handsome Vince Edwards soared to stardom as Casey.

tirely replace family sit-coms, but there was a new fad—single parent families. The fathers and mothers were always widowed. Divorced parents did not hit the screen until the 1970s.

My Three Sons, a very successful comedy, starred Fred MacMurray. He raised his sons with the help of a housekeeping grandfather (William Frawley), later replaced by an uncle (William Demarest).

Two-parent families did not disappear altogether. *The Dick Van Dyke Show* was one of the top ten programs. In the series Van Dyke played a writer for TV shows. His wife was played by Mary Tyler Moore, who frequently sighed, "Oh, Rob."

Comedy filled the air throughout the '60s.

OXYGEN, QUICK

Because doctors deal with life and death situations, medical programs are a natural for TV. They provide suspense and emotion-packed moments. The first medical show was *Medic* (1954), starring Richard Boone.

Medical programs reached epidemic proportions during the 1960s. The usual pattern for medical shows is to team up an old crusty doctor with a young intern. Two enormously popular doctors began their TV practices in 1961—Dr. Kildare and Ben Casey.

Marcus Welby, M.D. teamed Robert Young as an old-fashioned family doctor, Welby, with James Brolin, playing a young modern doctor who made house calls on his motorcycle. The program was an immediate hit. The sympathetic image that Young portrayed so well on *Father Knows Best* worked again in his role as Welby.

Like hospitals, courtrooms are filled with heart-rending events. The best-known lawyer to practice on TV was *Perry Mason.* Raymond Burr starred as Mason. He was helped by his secretary, Della Street (Barbara Hale) and a private eye, Paul Drake (William Hopper). Each week Mason faced D.A. Burger and each week Mason won. His trademark was to free his client by naming the real murderer, who conveniently sat at the back of the courtroom.

Perry Mason ran from 1957 to 1966 and is now syndicated. Local stations run the 245 episodes again and again. *Perry Mason* was based on the character created by writer Erle Stanley Gardner.

The Defenders was a highly respected law series in which controversial issues such as capital punishment were handled. E. G. Marshall and Robert Reed starred as a father/son lawyer team.

SPINACH POWER

Prime time for children is Saturday morning. That's when cartoons, cartoons, cartoons are aired. Produced originally for movie theaters, cartoons moved to TV by the droves because children and advertisers love them. The cartoons are filled with lovable, laughable animals such as Donald Duck, Bugs Bunny, and Tom and Jerry.

From the 1960s to the present the same cartoon characters have dominated the TV screen. Their personalities have changed little, but the plots were updated. For example, Yogi Bear originally lived in Jellystone National Park where he drove the forest ranger wild with his antics. Now he jets around in space on Yogi's Spacerace.

Fred Flintstone, the Pink Panther, Popeye, the super-heroes, Scooby Doo, and others are in "new" versions of their cartoon shows.

These are a small sampling of the weekly cartoon series.

In sharp contrast to those children's programs filled with noise and mayhem are *Captain Kangaroo* and *Mister Rogers' Neighborhood*. The Captain first came to TV in 1955 and he's still on the air entertaining preschoolers every weekday morning. Captain Kangaroo

Top left: Captain Kangaroo in his red blazer is easily recognized by children. One of the changes over the years was his switch from a uniform and a cap to his jacket. Old-timers recall that Bob Keeshan, better known as the Captain, was the first Clarabell on *The Howdy Doody Show. Bottom left:* Mister Rogers' puppet friends live in the Neighborhood-of-Make-Believe. *Right:* Popeye's punch packs a wallop when he eats his spinach. Originally introduced as a comic strip character in 1929, he was responsible for a 39 percent increase in the sale of spinach between 1929 and 1933.

Above: Hee Haw was a country-western comedy show on CBS from 1969 to 1970. Buck Owens and Roy Clark were the co-hosts. Despite high ratings, *Hee Haw* was canceled because the network wanted to drop its rural-image programs. Production for local stations continued with sucess. *Right:* Standing between Dick and Tom Smothers is Pat Paulsen, a regular on *The Smothers Brothers Comedy Hour.* The program was sixty minutes of madcap jokes and songs about religion, war, and politics —subjects that made the program controversial.

is friendly and soft-spoken. With the help of his friends Mr. Green Jeans, Dancing Bear, Dennis, Grandfather Clock, and puppets Mr. Moose and Bunny Rabbit, he appears in amusing situations, shows live animals, and tells stories.

Soft-spoken Fred Rogers invites the viewers into his home on *Mister Rogers' Neighborhood.* He talks to young children about their problems and worries. He demonstrates how to cope with worrisome situations such as a visit to a doctor.

SOCK IT TO ME

A powerhouse of talent, Carol Burnett starred in her own show for eleven years. Her antics, expressions and sight gags are hilarious. She developed several characters for her comedy routines, including a charwoman (cleaning woman) and Eunice, a neurotic.

Harvey Korman, Tim Conway, Lyle Waggoner, and Carol's look-alike Vicki Lawrence performed with her. Regularly Korman and Burnett played a married couple who argued about their liberated teen-ager (Lawrence).

Carol Burnett won several Emmy Awards and her program was still highly rated when she chose to quit in order to act in movies.

A time of unrest, the 1960s were ripe for jokes about politics and the American way of life. *Rowan and Martin's Laugh-In* was a madcap comedy hour. The skits, songs, dances, and standup routines made fun of anything and everything.

The regular cast members were a talented group including Lily Tomlin, Goldie Hawn, Joanne Worley, Alan Sues, Ruth Buzzi, Arte Johnson, and Gary Owens. Well-known guests such as John Wayne were "tricked" into saying the catchphrase "Sock it to me." A giant "hammer" socked them, and they fell through a trapdoor.

The Smothers Brothers Comedy Hour, like *Laugh-In,* was a tremendous hit. Religious jokes, comments about Viet Nam, and protest songs made Tommy and Dick Smothers controversial. They also annoyed the CBS censors, and after clashes with the network the show was canceled.

The first comedy-variety show starring a black performer was *The Flip Wilson Show* (1970–74). Flip Wilson often performed in skits as Geraldine Jones, a tough woman, and the Reverend Leroy of the Church of What's Happening Now.

As the times changed, the comedies changed.

"...ONE GIANT LEAP FOR MANKIND."

The most dramatic moments on TV during the 1960s were actual events. The networks brought us an astounding number of hours of news.

The year 1960 was the year of the Great Debates between John F. Kennedy and Richard M. Nixon, both candidates for the presidency. They agreed to four televised debates. Kennedy looked relaxed, self-assured, and handsome during the first debate. Nixon looked tired. The election was very close; Kennedy received 34,227,096 votes and Nixon 34,108,546. Many people believe that Nixon lost the election because his TV image was poor.

On November 22, 1963, President John F. Kennedy was killed by an assassin. Millions of Americans watched his funeral on TV. The day before the funeral a horrified public watched the shooting of the accused assassin, Lee Harvey Oswald, on live television.

The 1960s were a time of tragedy. We watched the funerals of civil rights leader Martin Luther King, Jr. and Senator Robert Kennedy. We watched racial riots, violence at the 1968 Democratic Convention, bombings of the Vietnam War, and anti-war rallies.

But TV also brought us the highest moments in the history of the U.S. space program. And satellites made possible live transmission from abroad.

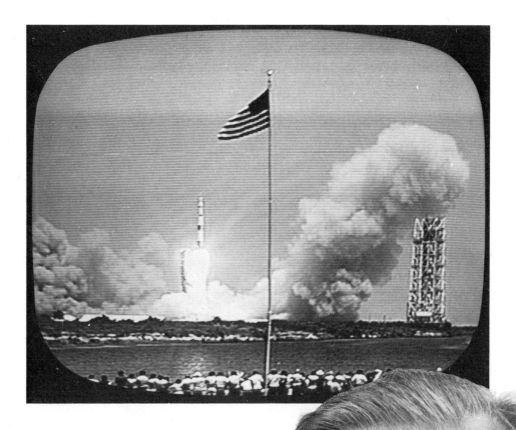

Above: TV presented an incredible number of hours covering the space achievements of the United States. Each of the networks developed experts in space coverage. *Right:* Walter Cronkite is the number-one anchorman in the country. He joined the CBS News team in 1950 as a correspondent and moved up to anchor in 1962. He's covered conventions, blast-offs, funerals, inaugurations—all of the major events at home and abroad. According to one poll, he's the "most trusted man in America."

Archie (Carroll O'Connor) referred to his wife Edith (Jean Stapleton) as a "dingbat." Their daughter Gloria (Sally Struthers) and her husband Michael (Rob Reiner) generally opposed Archie on every major issue. Despite all the shouting and insults, the family was very closely knit.

PART V
THE '70S:
THE SPIN-OFF
ERA

In the 1970s TV programs were similar to those of the 1960s—police and action shows, sit-coms, soap operas, all the standard fare—but with one noticeable difference. More violence and sex filled the screen, to the point that groups such as the PTA pressured the networks to tone down the mayhem. Once-taboo subjects such as divorce became common.

In response to the civil rights movement and the women's liberation movement, women and blacks starred in new programs and moved into the newsrooms as reporters.

The greatest innovation of the 1970s was the miniseries. For the first time in TV history, adaptations of books were aired on consecutive nights.

Noncommercial television, through the Public Broadcasting Service, attracted attention by airing several excellent dramatic series.

Above: most of the action on *The Mary Tyler Moore Show* took place in the WJM-TV newsroom where Mary played a newscaster. She's seen here with Lou Grant (who went on to star in his own award-winning show), and Gavin McLeod (who later starred in *Love Boat*). *Right:* Henry Winkler as the Fonz on *Happy Days* attracted millions of fans. The role was originally a minor one and no one expected the Fonz to become a cult figure.

MARY TYLER
AND MORE

Women in sit-coms were generally portrayed as housewives or widows. Then came *The Mary Tyler Moore Show.* Mary Tyler Moore played Mary Richards, who was single and over thirty. She was a spunky news producer for WJM-TV in Minneapolis. *The Mary Tyler Moore Show* was notable for its excellent writing and superb casting. The supporting characters later starred in their own programs, known as spin-offs.

Almost all of the action occurred in the newsroom or in Mary's apartment. Rhoda Morgenstern (Valerie Harper) and the owner, Phyllis (Cloris Leachman), lived in Mary's apartment building. Both actresses provided a lot of laughs, and they subsequently played the title roles in the shows *Rhoda* and *Phyllis.*

Rhoda was launched with the leading character's marriage to Joe Gerard, played by David Groh. As a married woman, Rhoda did not seem as funny as before, so she was "separated" and then "divorced."

At the height of its popularity Mary Tyler Moore terminated the show to star in a new variety program, *Mary,* which failed. It was pulled out of the schedule for revamping and returned as *The Mary Tyler Moore Hour,* which also failed.

All in the Family was a landmark sit-com because it used mature themes and frank language. Archie Bunker, the central character, is known in every house. He is a working-class bigot, who lives in Queens. His daughter and her husband live next door. His son-in-law, Michael, whom he calls "meathead," is a liberal. He and Archie do not agree on anything.

The Jeffersons and *Maude* were based on characters that originally appeared on *All in the Family. Good Times,* in turn, was based on a character from *Maude.*

Edith, Archie Bunker's wife, has a cousin Maude who is a loud-mouth liberal. The program *Maude* often dealt with controversial issues within the framework of comedy. Beatrice Arthur won an Emmy for her role as Maude. Bill Macy played her husband.

The Jeffersons were black neighbors of the Bunkers until they moved uptown to a fancy apartment. The husband, George, owns a chain of dry-cleaning stores, and the plots usually revolve around one of his schemes to attract new customers. Louise is his long-suffering wife, and Lionel, their son, is married to Jennie Willis. Her mother is black, her father white. A bi-racial couple on TV had been unheard of in a comedy.

Good Times stars Esther Rolle as the head of a poor urban black family. She was the maid Florida on *Maude.* The children are played by Ja'net DuBois, Ralph Carter, BernNadette Stanis, and Jimmie Walker, who soared to stardom.

Sit-coms flourished. They featured all types of arrangements and family situations. Two divorced men live together in *The Odd Couple.* Felix (Tony Randall) is compulsively neat; Oscar (Jack Klugman) is a slob. The comedy revolves around the differences in their personalities.

Happy Days is representative of the 1950s nostalgia craze that swept the nation. Arthur Fonzerelli (played by Henry Winkler), better known as "the Fonz," was a supporting character, but he stole the show. Fonzie is a know-it-all dropout. Thumbs pointed up, he's heard saying, "AHHHHHH."

A spin-off of *Happy Days, Laverne and Shirley* became an immediate hit. The title characters are two wacky women who share an apartment in Milwaukee during the 1950s. Penny Marshall and Cindy Williams star as the roommates.

Mork, who's from the planet of Ork, once dropped in on the *Happy Days* gang. He became the central character on *Mork and Mindy*, an instant hit in 1978. Mork, played by the zany comedian Robin Williams, learns about life on Earth by copying others.

(74)

Left: **Robin Williams stars as Mork and Pam Dawber as Mindy in the hilarious sci-fi spoof *Mork and Mindy*, which premiered in 1978. *Mork and Mindy* was an instant hit. *Below:* his role as one of the Sweathogs in *Welcome Back, Kotter*, catapulted John Travolta (top left) to a movie career and fame.**

Bottom left: Michael Landon as Charles Ingalls provides the wholesome image necessary for *Little House on the Prairie.* *Top left:* The Waltons pose for a picture. They are a poor but happy rural family living in Appalachia during the 1930s. Often Grandpa Walton (Will Geer) provided words of wisdom. *Right:* Family, a sentimental drama-comedy, was introduced in 1976 as a mini-series. In this family, mother knows best. Sada Thompson as the mother dispenses advice and understanding to her divorced daughter (Meredith Baxter-Birney), dropout son (Gary Frank), and teenage daughter (Kristy McNichol). Father is also wise; he's played by James Broderick.

MA, PA:
THOSE WERE THE DAYS

Two highly sentimental dramas became surprise hits: *Little House on the Prairie* and *The Waltons.* They represented old-fashioned values and portrayed families with strong fathers, devoted mothers, active grandparents, and well-behaved children.

Based on a series of books by Laura Ingalls Wilder, *Little House on the Prairie* traces the struggles of the Ingalls family in Minnesota during the 1870s. The daughter Laura acts as the narrator. The family faces death, blindness, storms, droughts, and corruption.

The Waltons fits no formula. There is no sex or violence, but it soared to the top of the ratings. John-Boy is the oldest child of a family living in Appalachia. He wants to be a writer, and he tells his family's story. He was played by Richard Thomas. When Richard Thomas left the show in 1977, John-Boy left "to go to college." Thomas still makes guest appearances occasionally.

Family dramas and sit-coms set in modern times continued as well. The American family grew smaller during the 1970s, but TV families grew larger. *Eight Is Enough* is about the Bradford family. The father works as a reporter; he's played by Dick Van Patten, whose first TV role was a son on the sit-com *Mama.*

The Partridge Family was a musical sit-com about five brothers and sisters who became a professional rock group. Shirley Jones played the widowed mother, who managed the house and the group. Of the child performers, David Cassidy became a superstar.

The Brady Bunch (1964–74) featured a young widow with three daughters who married a widower with three sons. The comedy revolved around the chaos of large family living. Robert Reed starred as the architect father. Florence Henderson played the mother.

WHO LOVES YA, BABY?

Bang! Hold it right there.

Night after night police dramas fill the screen. There are two kinds of cops: the maverick, break-the-rules, violent policemen and the "new breed," who don't want to shoot.

Kojak was a program about a break-the-rules cop working in New York. Bald Telly Savalas gave life to the character of Lieutenant Theo Kojak, a man of Greek descent. He chewed lollipops, wore elegant clothes, and often exclaimed, "Who loves ya, baby?" *Kojak* was an enormously popular adult police series.

Baretta was also a maverick. As an undercover cop, Tony Baretta ignored standard police procedures. The criminals were captured after a careening car chase or shootout. Criticized for its violence, *Baretta* went off the air in 1978.

Police Story (1973–77) portrayed police work more realistically. It was an anthology series with no single star. *Police Woman* was a spin-off. Angie Dickinson played Sergeant Suzanne ("Pepper") Anderson. She was a divorced and attractive undercover detective with the Los Angeles Police Department.

Starsky and Hutch was distinguished as a very violent police drama. Paul Michael Glaser and David Soul starred as the good-buddy police team.

The Rookies represented the new breed. Three young officers fought crime in southern California. They were reluctant to use guns.

The most unique detective is *Columbo,* played excellently by Peter Falk. Dressed in a wrinkled raincoat, he looks like an untidy, fumbling fool. His mind, however, is razor sharp. He always catches the culprit, but never fires a gun. He's known for saying, "Just one more thing. . . ."

Quincy originated on the *NBC Sunday Mystery Movie.* Jack Klugman stars in the role of a medical examiner who is never satisfied until he solves each mystery about a dead man or woman.

Above left: Charlie's Angels are three private detectives who work for Charlie Townsend. He's heard but never seen. The angels here are Kate Jackson, Jaclyn Smith, and Cheryl Ladd, who replaced Farrah Fawcett-Majors. The action-adventure plus the sex appeal made *Charlie's Angels* an instant hit. *Above right:* Columbo (Peter Falk) discovers every clue, no matter how small. He pieces together the tiniest shreds of evidence to trap the killer. *Right:* David Soul and Paul Michael Glazer, relatively unknown to TV audiences, became stars as police buddies on *Starsky and Hutch.* Premiering in 1975, it quickly climbed in the ratings and established itself as a violent drama.

Above right: the regulars on *The Electric Company* make reading fun. Fargo North spoofs detectives as he fumbles through code words. Spiderman stories are read. The skits are lively and the program is successful because it uses characters and situations that children enjoy watching. Rita Moreno (wearing cap) acts as a director. *Left:* Big Bird is the most popular of all the *Sesame Street* characters.

OH, THERE YOU ARE, MR. SNUFFLE-UPAGUS

Sesame Street revolutionized children's programming when it began in 1969. The object of the show was to teach preschool children numbers, letters, shapes, and values. There were stories, games, skits, and "commercials" for numbers. The fast pace of the program was a contrast to preschool programs such as *Romper Room* and *Captain Kangaroo.*

Adults, children, and muppets live on Sesame Street. The muppets include Bert and Ernie, Cookie Monster, Oscar the Grouch, and Big Bird. Not too bright, Big Bird makes mistakes, asks a lot of questions and gets upset. His friend is Mr. Snuffle-upagus, a huge, elephant-like creature.

All of the characters help children with their problems and fears by experiencing the same emotions as kids themselves.

Beginning in 1976, Jim Henson created new muppets. They starred in their own show. Each week *The Muppets* features a guest and the regular puppet cast: Kermit, Fuzzy Bear, Gonzo, and Miss Piggy.

Saturday mornings are still dominated by cartoons. Old favorites like Popeye and Mighty Mouse race across the screen. Super-heroes are often the stars of cartoons: Superman, Batman, Wonder Woman.

Once a month the *ABC Afterschool Specials* presents top-flight movies or dramas for children. *NBC Special Treat* also airs quality films for kids.

The lack of high-quality programs aimed at children led a group of four women in Massachusettes to form an organization called Action for Children's Television (ACT) in 1968. ACT's goals are to improve television programs for children and to eliminate commercials from children's shows. Now there are thousands of ACT members all over the country.

ACROSS THE WAVES

A number of British television shows came across the waves in the mid 1970s, and they were aired by the Public Broadcasting Service. They were so successful in the ratings that the networks were rivaled by non-commercial TV during prime time.

The most successful dramatic series from the BBC (British Broadcasting Corporation) was *Upstairs, Downstairs,* a sub-series of *Masterpiece Theater.* Set in England, the series opened in 1903. It focused on the lives of the wealthy Bellamy family and their servants, who lived in the quarters downstairs. It traced their lives through World War I and the Depression to the year 1931. In a remarkable turn of events, CBS tried to imitate *Upstairs, Downstairs* with *Beacon Hill,* a failure.

The Adams Chronicles, produced in the United States for the Bicentennial, was a historical drama series. Four generations of the Adams family were traced, beginning with John Adams (later President John Adams) and his wife, Abigail, in 1750. The critics praised *The Adams Chronicles,* and it drew the largest audiences ever for a PBS presentation.

Following the success of series on non-commercial stations, the commercial networks programmed mini-series. Popular novels such as *The Blue Knight, QB VII,* and *Wheels* were adapted for TV.

Roots was a milestone. ABC stunned the TV industry when it aired this eight-part mini-series on consecutive nights. *Roots* was based on Alex Haley's book in which he traced his family's history beginning with Kunta Kinte, an African brought to the United States as a slave. He tried to escape from the plantation over and over again but never lost hope of escaping for good.

Roots scored the highest ratings in TV history for an entertainment program. Its popularity was remarkable because the heroes were black and the villains mostly white.

The enormous success of *Roots* led to *Roots: The Next Generations.*

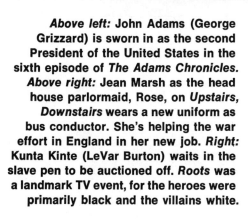

Above left: John Adams (George Grizzard) is sworn in as the second President of the United States in the sixth episode of *The Adams Chronicles.* *Above right:* Jean Marsh as the head house parlormaid, Rose, on *Upstairs, Downstairs* wears a new uniform as bus conductor. She's helping the war effort in England in her new job. *Right:* Kunta Kinte (LeVar Burton) waits in the slave pen to be auctioned off. *Roots* was a landmark TV event, for the heroes were primarily black and the villains white.

Above: Victory at Entebbe was a dramatization of an Israeli raid on Entebbe Airport in Uganda on July 4, 1976, to rescue a hijacked plane. In the Military Planning Room, Shomrun (Harris Yulin) presents his plan of the rescue mission to Peres (Burt Lancaster).
Below: Eleanor and Franklin starred Ed Herrmann and Jane Alexander in a four-hour series about the lives and careers of President Franklin Delano Roosevelt and his wife.

FACT
OR
FICTION?

A fad began in the late 1970s for dramas based on historical events. They were called docu-dramas, and they were often more fiction than fact.

Richard Nixon resigned the presidency of the United States as a result of the Watergate scandals. *Washington: Behind Closed Doors* was a drama series based on the events leading to Nixon's downfall.

Holocaust caused the most controversy. It was a four-part series dramatizing the events of World War II in Nazi Germany, where millions of Jews were put in concentration camps and executed. The plot was told through two families, a Jewish family and the family of a Nazi Gestapo officer.

Some critics said it failed to capture the importance of the world's greatest tragedy. Other critics praised it. Approximately 120 million Americans watched *Holocaust.*

Docu-dramas about John F. Kennedy's assassination (*The Trial of Lee Harvey Oswald*), about well-known performers (*Elvis*), and important leaders (*Martin Luther King, Jr.*) are just a few of the events dramatized on TV.

As the docu-dramas increased, the documentaries decreased. Documentaries rarely attract large audiences.

Of the news magazine programs, only *60 Minutes* achieves high ratings. Each week there are three documentary segments tackling controversial issues and unusual news items. Mike Wallace and Harry Reasoner were the co-editors when the program premiered in 1968.

CONCLUSION: LOOKING AHEAD

The first fifty years of television
revolutionized American life.
Now TV itself is on the threshold
of a development that will change it.
Videotape recorders allow us to
tape one program while watching another.
The ratings will therefore hold less meaning.
We will also buy prerecorded videotapes
just as we buy records or cassettes.

How much TV will change is uncertain,
but everyone expects television to
become an even more important part
of our lives in the next fifty years.

BIBLIOGRAPHY

Barnouw, Erik. *Tube of Plenty.* New York: Oxford University Press, 1975.

Brown, Les, ed. *The New York Times Encyclopedia of Television.* New York: Quadrangle/The New York Times Book Co., 1977.

Cahn, William, and Rhoda Cahn. *A Pictorial History of the Great Comedians.* New York: Grosset and Dunlap, 1970.

Fireman, Judy, ed. *TV Book.* New York: Workman Publishing, 1977.

Glut, Donald F., and Jim Harmon. *The Great Television Heroes.* Garden City, New York: Doubleday, 1975.

Greenfield, Jeff. *Television: The First Fifty Years.* New York: Harry N. Abrams, 1977.

Horwitz, James. *They Went Thataway.* New York: Dutton, 1976.

Sennett, Ted. *Your Show of Shows.* New York: Macmillan, 1977.

Settel, Irving, and William Laas. *A Pictorial History of Television.* New York: Grosset and Dunlap, 1969.

Shulman, Arthur, and Roger Youman. *How Sweet It Was.* New York: Bonanza Books, 1965.

Terrace, Vincent. *The Complete Encyclopedia of Television Programs 1947–1976.* New York: A. S. Barnes, 1976.

Wilk, Max. *The Golden Age of Television: Notes from the Survivors.* New York: Delacorte Press, 1976.

World Book Encyclopedia, Vol. 19. Chicago: Field Enterprises Educational Corp., 1972.

INDEX